For A. O.
J. P.

First edition 2004

Library of Congress Cataloging-in-Publication Data is available.

Library of Congress Catalog Card Number 99-057125

ISBN 1-56402-679-5

2 4 6 8 10 9 7 5 3 1

Printed in China

This book was typeset in Godlike.
The illustrations were done in watercolor and ink.

Candlewick Press
2067 Massachusetts Avenue
Cambridge, Massachusetts 02140

visit us at www.candlewick.com

LOVE THAT BABY!

A book about babies for
new brothers, sisters, cousins, and friends

Kathryn Lasky   illustrated by Jennifer Plecas

CANDLEWICK PRESS
CAMBRIDGE, MASSACHUSETTS

HELLO,

BABY!

A baby is born!

She's reddish pink or brownish red.

She's bald or has a few spikes of hair,

or maybe a little dab of fuzz or one corkscrew curl.

She may be your new cousin or your friend's new sister.

She may even be your own new sister.

At first it might seem like all
your baby does is eat and sleep.

You used to do that too.

But babies are fascinating. Just watch one!

WIDE-AWAKE BABY

Have you ever watched a baby wake up?
His little mouth stretches from
a little O to a big wide yawn.

Your baby might be
very happy when he wakes up.
When babies are very, very happy,
they kick their legs and wave their arms.
Babies love to watch their own hands.
They suck their fingers and gum their knuckles.
Sometimes they even try to suck their toes!

It's really exciting when a baby
figures out how to roll over.
Now he can look at what he wants—
the ceiling, the walls, a special toy.

Newborn babies have to nurse . . .

YUM

Eating is what babies do best.
Newborn babies snack all the time,
but they only have one
kind of food—
milk!
They either nurse
or take a bottle
or do both.

or drink from a bottle.

When a baby eats banana slices, it's a mess.

The baby puts the slices on her head. Then she takes them off.

YUM

When babies get a little bit older,
they start to eat solid food.
Since babies don't have any teeth,
they eat soft, mushy food
like strained vegetables and baby cereal.
Yum!
Babies are very messy when they eat,
and they don't even care.

Some older babies like to stick Cheerios on their noses . . .

Mom!

or smear pudding between their toes.

*Then she squashes
them in her fist.
Then she puts them
behind her ear.*

*Finally
she swallows some
of them.*

BABY TALK

Babies babble a lot. It's their way of talking.
It doesn't matter where a baby comes from—
America or Africa or Asia or Europe.
Baby babble is the same in all languages.

When your baby babbles, babble right back.
Babies love this. They think it's a real conversation.
And it kind of is.

Babies are also very good at smiling.
When you talk to your baby and she smiles,
it makes you want to keep talking to her.
Smile talk, smile talk, back and forth.
Babies get a lot of attention this way!

Newborn babies make cooing sounds
when they are feeling happy.
Older babies gurgle and chortle.
That is how babies laugh, not *ha ha*.
Babies have a really good sense of humor.
They laugh when something's funny or a little bit weird.

BABY CRIES

(or Crybabies)

Babies cry because they can't tell you
when something's wrong.
They can't say, "My tummy hurts,"
or "I want that toy," or "I hate applesauce,"
or "I miss my mommy."

When babies cry, they open their mouths so wide!
Their mouths stretch into
huge lopsided black holes,
and they scream enormous screams.

If you listen carefully, you can tell that
your baby has different kinds of cries.
She might whine or whimper or scream.
Sometimes you can even tell by the sound
of your baby's cry what it is she wants.

You can help feed her, or cuddle her,
or just talk softly to her.
Even if your baby doesn't stop crying,
she will still know that you are near
and that you love her.

Some Ways to Help Quiet a Crying Baby

*Try looking in
the mirror.*

Sing a little song.

*Turn on a
water faucet.*

*Rock, rock, rock.
Bounce, bounce, bounce.*

*Grab an adult
and go for a car ride.*

Pace, pace, pace . . .

Peekaboo

Babies love to play peekaboo.
When you hide your face,
babies think you've disappeared.
They'll want to try this trick themselves.
It seems like baby magic to them.

Clapping

Babies love to try to clap.
Sometimes their hands clap together
just right and sometimes they miss.
You can see that babies are thinking
when they're trying to clap.
They look very serious.
Clapping can be as hard for a baby
as hitting a baseball is for a big kid.

This Little Piggy

This little piggy went to the movies.
This little piggy stayed home.
This little piggy had popcorn.
This little piggy had none . . .

Babies also like the toe-piggy game.
They think it is very funny.
You can have fun too,
by making up silly words.

Banging

Babies like banging even more
than clapping. They like to make
thumps and bumps,
bangs and clatters.
Build some block towers
for a baby to knock down.
They love the crash!
It makes them feel big, powerful,
and noisy—just plain terrific.

WET BABIES

Babies are wettest when they take baths.
Their hair gets slicked down
like wet paint splashes on their heads.
Their eyelashes turn spiky,
with water drops in between.

Some babies like baths.

Some babies hate baths.

Some babies get
wild and splash.

Some babies get mad
and howl in the water.

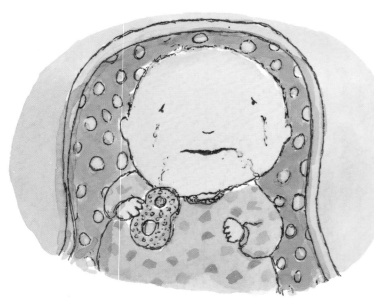

Babies' cheeks also get wet when they cry.
Their chins get wet when they drool.
If your baby grabs something of yours,
chances are it will go right in her mouth
and come back to you all wet and yucky.

Babies' bottoms are usually
the wettest part of them because of peeing.

Babies pee in their diapers because
they don't know or care about toilets—
or even at first about being dry!

SLEEPY BABIES

Babies can get sleepy anytime—
in backpacks, in cars, even eating lunch.

Babies sleep in different ways.
Some nap a lot.
And others don't.
Your baby might wake up
often in the night to be fed
or changed or cuddled.
Or he might sleep soundly
all night long.

Babies are only babies for a very short time.
It is a wonderful time, even though babies
can be sticky and icky and slimy,
with bananas stuck behind their ears.
Before you know it, your baby will stop babbling
and start talking. "No!" is a favorite baby word.
But she'll still laugh when she plays with you,
and she'll still love you just the same—
and you'll still love that baby!

Bye-bye, baby!